ENERGETIC BOUNDARIES 101

Joanna Schmidt

Mike,
Thanks for your
Good work in the
world And with
animals.
♡ Joanna

ENERGETIC BOUNDARIES 101

To my teachers and allies,
thank you.

Contents

Introduction

Welcome! I am glad you have picked up a copy of *Energetic Boundaries 101*.

This book covers the basics of creating an energetic boundary and many of the things we do with our energy when we are not working with clear and loving energetic boundaries.

The concepts and exercises in this book are the foundation of a large body of work on energetic boundaries. This work is an accumulation of my original work and a few time tested centering techniques I've assembled over the course of my twenty-year healing practice.

At the start of my career, I became increasingly frustrated by the lack of prevention and wellness resources for empathic and energy-sensitive people. Too many of the energetic tools created to support sensitive people, unfortunately also place us in the role of victim by encouraging disassociation from the very people and situations that could most benefit from our gifts and help us personally grow and evolve. Even energy protection techniques, created with the intent of helping us feel safe in the world, place us in the role of persecutor by labeling normal emotions and relatively healthy energy patterns as toxic and negative.

With my frustration increasing, I chose to reevaluate how we can approach and interact with our energy, our body, and our world and create energetic boundaries that honor all of life. It was out of my desire to transform these outdated ways of looking and working with energy that this work was born.

At the core of this practice is learning how to root our body and subtle energy in the present moment. As a practice, aligning our being in the present can take courage and effort as we often rely on leaving, shrinking, creating walls, or even hiding when things get difficult. It may also require us to take responsibility in how our energy interacts with others and transform any patterns of blame and judgment of others we may carry.

In writing this book, I have purposely used the word *energy* rather than *soul, spirit, aura, consciousness,* and so forth, in an effort to create a practice that can be as nondenominational and as kid-friendly as possible. While you are reading, I encourage you to substitute the language that most resonates for you.

I also invite you to read with an open heart and mind, as this book challenges many of the ways we have been taught to perceive and work with energy and interact with others.

Many of the techniques I describe can feel challenging to maintain at first. I encourage you to keep practicing. Many of us have spent a lifetime mastering the ways of interacting with others as illustrated in the energetic survival spectrum. It is our norm, our primary way of being in the world. Learning to recognize these often subtle patterns, and transform them, takes courage and much love and gratitude for who we are, our story, and those around us.

It is my hope that the practices shared in this book will help you to feel safe to shine your light in the world. The world needs sensitive people to feel empowered and share their unique gifts, now more than ever.

Shine on,

Joanna

We Are Brilliant Beings

As humans we have a rich and dynamic being that consists of both physical matter and energy. Our earthly physical body and our spirit body both contain a vast amount of information that helps make up who we are, including our personality, the divine mission for our life, and how to go about achieving it.

We are brilliant beings

Our physical bodies are amazing!

Within our physical being is a powerful mix of earth matter, water, and stardust. This amazing earthly mix within our cells, bones, muscles, and blood is a rich, dynamic pool of information about us, our ancestors, and our world.

The earth matter, water, and stardust within us did not start their journey with us. The water within our bodies has been a part of oceans and rainstorms, has lived within trees, plants, and other animals, before finding its way to us. Imagine the stories held in each glass of water you drink!

The earthly matter, too, has had a long journey before meeting us. It has been soil, and earthworms, before growing into a tree to grow the apple we had with our lunch.

And think of the journeys the stardust has had as it floated through space before forming our little planet Earth and helping to form our bodies!

These amazing physical bodies of ours hold a treasure trove of information about our ancestors, our planet, and our universe, all of it helping to make up our unique selves.

Our physical body radiating its amazing story

Showering your physical body with attention

In this exercise, give yourself plenty of time to listen to your inner being by using all of your senses. Follow your breath inward to listen to and feel the subtle movements created by your breath, as well as the many inner pulses and rhythms that your body creates.

1. Start by feeling the movement within your body created by your breath. You do not need to take more air into your lungs; simply listen inward, intent-fully, to the rich inner world within your own being.

2. Trace the curves of your body from head to toes, from inside your own skin, with your awareness, breath, and attention.

3. Notice how many different rhythms and pulses you can feel in addition to your breath and heartbeat.

4. Notice the areas in your body where you feel more heat and the areas where you have a harder time feeling anything at all.

5. If an area of discomfort is holding most of your attention, that is okay. Try listening to what that area has to say rather than blocking it out.

6. Simply feel your breath from inside your own body, how it moves through your lungs and belly, and how it comes into contact with each and every aspect of your physical body.

7. Shower your whole being with gratitude for carrying you through your day and holding you while you dream.

8. When you are ready to finish, allow your inner senses to soften as your awareness once again includes both your inner being and the world around you.

Our brilliant energy body

In addition to our physical body, we also have an energy body.

Depending on what you believe (and there are many possibilities!), we are also made up of a dynamic electromagnetic field. Some call this energy body *spirit* or *soul*, and others call it *consciousness*. Our energy body surrounds and works in tandem with our physical body and is a brilliant mix made from our light, vibration, and energy, containing a ton of information about who we are and our life's mission.

If we believe that our energy body is a result of our consciousness, that means our energy body is made from all of the brilliant things we have learned, experienced, and contemplated in our life.

If we believe in reincarnation, that means this energy of ours also contains everywhere we have *ever* been!

If we are informed by the shamanic quantum physics school of thought, this energy of ours also contains everything we have ever been or *ever* will go and be!

And if we believe in a higher power or universal truth … this colorful energy body of ours is our direct connection to Source or God.

This is a powerful concoction!

*Our physical and energetic
bodies radiating together*

Getting to know your energy body

Much as you listened inward to your physical body in the last exercise, you can use your inner senses to feel your energy body. Learning how to feel and sense your energy body will help you create and maintain energy boundaries. The more you can feel your energy body, the easier it will be to know how and where to focus your repair efforts when there is a breach.

1. Start by feeling into your physical body using your breath. Starting with your physical body will help anchor everything you feel in tangible, physical reality.

2. Pay attention to the sensations you feel just outside your skin. When you feel ready, follow these sensations out about 3 feet from your physical body, to the natural edge of where your energy stops and the rest of the world begins.

3. Notice the different sensations you feel while focused on feeling your energy body. Just like your physical body, your energy body is full of its own rhythms, pulses, and temperature differences. When exploring your energy body you may feel, see, or otherwise sense different aspects of your being. Explore how many different ways you can feel and experience your energy body.

4. After giving yourself plenty of time to explore, take a few soft breaths to reintegrate your physical and energy bodies.

5. Finish by fully reconnecting and offering your gratitude to your physical body, the earth, and the space around you.

Tip: If you feel spacey or as if you are floating, you may have gone too far outside of your physical body. Come back by following your breath home. You can feel into your energy body while remaining rooted within your physical body. This can take some practice, however!

Our body's captain: our awareness

If our physical and energy bodies have a captain, it is our awareness. Our awareness is the aspect of us that is able to pay attention and organize all that happens within our being and the world around us. (For more on this, see *Basic Psychic Development* by John Friedlander and Gloria Hemsher, 2012.)

Ideally this aspect of our being remains situated right at the center of our head, within the pituitary gland—perfectly centered, like a captain in a captain's seat.

Getting to know our awareness

We can feel our awareness using our inner senses. Some people report that it feels spongy, soft, and cloudlike, while others describe it as concrete, smooth, and solid, like a marble. When our awareness is not in the captain's seat in the center of our head, we can most often find it just forward, above, behind, or to one side of our head.

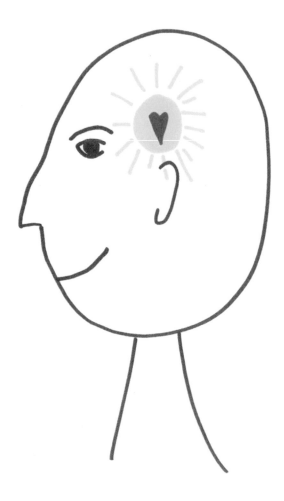

*Centering our awareness in
the center of our head*

Wandering awareness

Our awareness is in the habit of wandering off as it follows our thoughts, and this presents a challenge. Without an energetic boundary in place to remind our awareness to stay home, it will often leap from one situation to another, in and out of the past and future, as it follows our thoughts from one thing to the next. Our awareness can also jump in and out of the personal space of others before we even notice!

When our awareness is busy running all over the place, we can feel spacey, or the world can feel very loud, fast, and overwhelming. In some cases we can even feel like we have had a visit with a friend, just by thinking of them.

While an impromptu visit with a friend may sound like a good thing, when our awareness is running all over town our energy boundaries are nonexistent. And to make matters even more challenging, we lose the ability to pay attention to all of the wonderful things that our body and spirit offer, including our intuition, our inner senses, and full participation in the present moment.

Learning to work with your awareness

In this exercise you will take your time to explore with curiosity what your awareness feels like and where it hangs out, such as in front of, behind, or above your head, or perhaps very far away. Learning to sense what your awareness feels like and its location can help you center it as you progress in creating your energy boundaries. As with the other exercises, this is an in-your-body experience. If you feel floaty, simply follow your breath back home to your body.

1. Start by turning inward and feeling your physical body and the movement within your being created by your breath.

2. Using your natural inner senses, notice where you feel your awareness. It can be helpful to first notice how and where you feel your thoughts, then follow them directly to your awareness. You might feel, see, or otherwise sense where your awareness is in relation to your head. Do your best to explore where your awareness is rather than try to change or fix it at this time.

3. Using your energetic palpation skills, notice what your awareness feels like. Is it spongy, soft, hard? Do you see a color or hear or sense a sound associated with your awareness?

4. Spend time exploring. Spend a few rounds of your breath just paying attention to how your awareness shifts and moves. Your awareness is a vital aspect of who you are, and learning to feel and work with it will help you in creating your energetic boundary.

Tip: It can be helpful and fun to draw a colorful sketch of the patterns you see and feel when tuning in with your awareness. This can also solidify the experience of feeling into such subtle energy.

O captain my captain!

Again, when our awareness is at home within our being, it functions much like the captain of a large ship. When sitting in the captain's chair, a ship's captain has access to information about depth, wind speed, and everything else that keeps the ship afloat. Our senses such as hearing, seeing, feeling, tasting, and smelling are like the captain's crew, running all over the ship collecting important information. When the captain of a large ship has to multitask and collect all of that information on their own, they will quickly fall behind in other important captain's duties.

When our awareness runs all over the place, it can feel like our ship is speeding along out of control!

In contrast, when our awareness is at home in the center of our head, working with all the tools it has at hand, the world feels slower; things move at a more relaxed pace. When our awareness is in the center of our head, even the most charged events or situations feel workable.

Ways to call our awareness home

There are many ways to bring our awareness back to the center of our head. A few examples:

- ♥ Envisioning our awareness like a marble on a large wooden track, rolling around along the track until it rolls right into the center of our head

- ♥ Envisioning our awareness as a captain and helping our captain find their way back to the captain's chair on the bridge of a ship

- ♥ Envisioning our awareness like a beautiful egg and softly placing it into a cozy woven nest within the center of our head

- ♥ Envisioning placing our mind into neutral instead of drive or reverse

Bringing your awareness home

It can take several tries to bring your awareness home and to feel comfortable staying within the center of your head. In this exercise, play with finding which of the visualizations offered on page 17 works best for you. As you become more practiced, play around with finding your own method.

1. Using your inner palpation skills, locate your awareness in relation to the center of your head. Is it just above, behind, or in front of your head?

2. Use a visualization (see page 17) to play with bringing your awareness home to the center of your head.

3. Once your awareness is centered, slowly open your eyes and practice staying centered while you notice the world around you. Explore how to see, listen, and engage with the world while your awareness remains in the center of your head. This can take some practice.

4. Use both your intention and your relaxed breath to support your awareness remaining in the center of your head. It can take practice to build up the energetic muscles to do this, but rest assured that regular practice will help shift the habits of a wandering awareness.

Tip: When your awareness returns to the center of your head, your physical posture may shift slightly to more of an upright, proper position. Your breathing may become more relaxed as well.

Our body + our energy = our unique essence

The combined force of our physical and energy bodies creates a vibration or a vibrational song that is unique to us. Our vibration is like our personal signature in the world that radiates who we are, our mood, our story, and what our mission is. No two beings radiate the same vibrational song! Our personal vibrational signature helps us attract and find exactly what we are looking for from moment to moment. It is like we are all wearing an invisible sandwich board that tells the world who we are and what we need in this moment for our continued learning, growth, and development.

All the emotions we feel, like joy, fear, anger, and love, also radiate out through our vibrational signature.

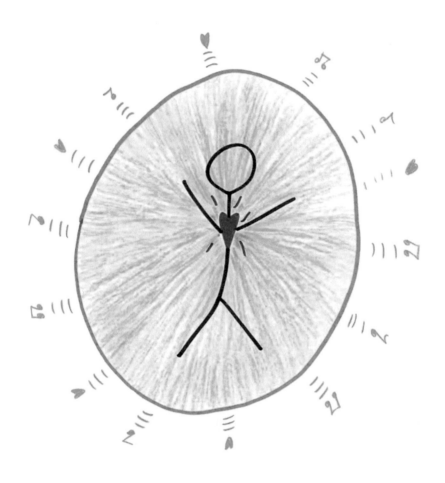

Radiating a unique vibration and song

WE ARE BRILLIANT BEINGS

Exploring your inner song and vibration

It is important to know what your own vibration feels like so that you can discern your energetic vibration from others. This requires a kind of inner listening, perceiving very subtle vibrations within your own being. Many people describe their inner song and vibration as a feeling rather than a sound. Your inner song creates a subtle vibration that can be sensed in both your physical and energetic bodies.

1. Allow several rounds of your breath to nourish your connection with your body. Give your mind permission to steady and relax.

2. Following your breath inward, feel your energy and physical body existing together in the present moment seamlessly—one working with the other, in harmony and perfect balance.

3. As you settle deeply into your own being, feel for your own inner energetic pulse or subtle rhythm using all of your inner senses. You can hear your inner song, feel it, sense it, see it, or simply know it is there. Do your best to stay rooted in the physical realm while listening and exploring.

4. Allow your awareness to soften and relax in the center of your head and to simply be in neutral curiosity as you listen and enjoy your own unique energetic inner song.

Tip: When feeling your inner song and vibration, it is common to feel very sleepy. If this happens for you, try this exercise several nights before bed, and increase the time you allot yourself for listening by five minutes each night. Get cozy while sitting upright in bed, and intend to spend about ten to fifteen minutes just listening to your own rhythms and inner song. If you fall asleep, that's okay! Try again the following night.

Feeling the rhythms of another's inner song

When we sense what others around us are feeling, we are sensing their unique vibrational signature.

When we have clear energy boundaries in place, this can be a wonderful thing. Being able to sense others' moods and unique vibrational signatures helps us to be empathetic to their needs, allowing us to be conscious, loving members of our family and community, and create a ton of healing in the world.

When we don't have a clear energetic boundary in place, things can get a little messy. The energy created by another's inner song can be drawn into our energy as though we are a thirsty sponge!

Energetic boundaries help us maintain our physical, emotional, and energetic autonomy so that we can live as the magical beings we are meant to be.

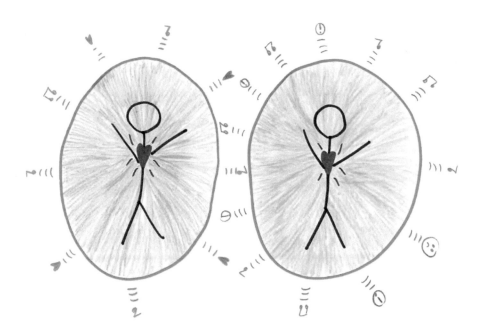

Two beings radiating their emotional songs:
one of joy, one of uncertainty

Our Wonderful Energetic Boundary

Let's think of our energetic boundary as an energy field that surrounds our physical and energy bodies. This transparent energy creates a container, allowing all that we are to reside in the same place at the same time. Without an energy boundary we are loose, floating around, mixing, mingling, and spilling all over the place with all the other folks who do not have an energy boundary in place.

Creating our own energetic boundary

At the foundation of our energetic boundary are our physical and energy bodies and the brilliant connection between the two. We need both our body and our energy working together as a team in the present moment to create a strong, loving, clear boundary.

To help us understand this invisible boundary that contains all of who we are, let's look at the formula that is needed to create one.

Energy boundary visualized with a blue line

The formula for an energy boundary:

Our body

+

Our energy

+

Our breath

+

Our presence in the present moment

+

Our love and gratitude

+

Our intent

———————————————

= Our energy boundary!

To create a boundary, we need each of these things, or our boundary will fall short.

Our Body + Our energy + Our Breath + our presence + our Love + Our intent = Our energy Boundary! ♥

The formula for an energy boundary

Boundaries are strong but also loving

When we first think of a boundary we often imagine a fence, wall, or other barrier with strong words like *keep out* written across the door.

However, this describes a wall, not a boundary. Boundaries are strong but also loving; they are fluid and stretchy like our physical body. They move with us and create space for all of our creative endeavors. Boundaries are like a pair of comfy, stretchy, flannel footie pajamas—as opposed to walls, which would look and feel like a rigid, tight, stiff chainmail coat of armor.

Walls are not boundaries

Part of a larger system

Our energetic boundary is part of a larger, cohesive system of boundaries that work together. On the physical level, we have our skin to keep things like germs out of our body. In our emotional being, we use our words and body language to define our emotional boundaries, and we also have energetic boundaries—what this book is all about! All of these boundaries work together to assist us in defining what is and is not us, and to live authentically.

These boundaries, when working together, keep us feeling secure and safe as we live our lives and do things like walk our dog, interact with friends, fall in love, and have spiritual experiences. With our boundaries in good shape and working well, we can even be around angry or stressed-out people and feel secure enough to offer them the healing words they may need to hear, without picking up their emotions or energy.

Two beings can be in the same place
without merging energy fields

Do boundaries separate us from those we love?

Our physical, emotional, and energetic bodies all create a vibration or inner song that is as unique as we are. When our individual vibration is contained within our energetic boundary, we can share space with others and still maintain our energetic and emotional autonomy and our unique vibration. We can hang with our cat, hold our sweetheart's hand, or be in a large crowd, and our vibration will remain ours and be true to our authentic inner song.

When our energy boundaries are in place, we can still relate to those around us, be intuitive, and even have spiritual experiences. Energetic boundaries help us maintain our own sovereignty so that we can get more out of each interaction and life experience.

As in the drawing to the right, we can be in the same place at the same time as another; while our energy and boundaries overlap, we are still within our own boundary. Many individuals with their own unique vibrations can overlap, like a freshly cooked stack of pancakes, and still remain individual. By contrast, without our energetic boundary, when we are in a crowd we become more like pancake batter, running all over the place and mixing in with the other pancakes.

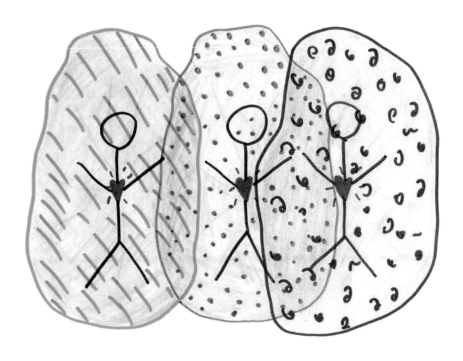

Many harmonies maintaining their own autonomy—different parts of the same song

Interacting with others with our energetic boundaries in place

The very edge of our energetic boundary is much like the sensitive skin of a drum. Small amounts of energy tapping on the skin can create a big vibration for the drum. Like the drum, the skin of our energetic boundary can stay strong while we feel, hear, and sense the vibration from the world around us.

When we do not have an energetic boundary, we bring the actual emotions and energy of others into our personal space in order to feel it. But with an energetic boundary in place, during our interactions we use the skin of our boundary to simply feel the energetic vibrational input on the edge of our boundary. We then simply translate the vibrational information, without bringing others' energy into our personal space.

In this way we can interact with those around us on both physical and energetic levels while maintaining our boundaries and personal space.

When we share a lovely experience with another, the interaction actually happens outside our boundary. We can visit with friends, hug, hold hands with others, and still maintain our emotional and energetic autonomy when we have a loving, clear energy boundary.

This allows each person to still have their own feelings, personal space, and energetic autonomy.

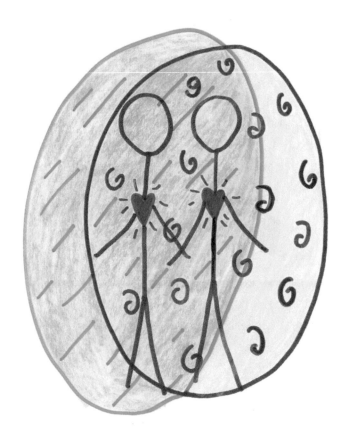

Two beings sharing a loving experience

Gouda or Swiss?

Let's envision our energy boundary as a beautiful block of Gouda wrapped in a smooth, brightly colored wax coating that keeps the cheese inside it safe, contained, and clean.

To envision what we look like without a boundary, imagine a block of Swiss cheese, full of holes and out of its wrapper, just sitting on the counter for bugs and other things to crawl right into.

Not such a pretty picture! The "Swiss cheese holes" in our energy are the places where we can't or don't know how to run our energy, presence, and breath. It is like we don't really exist in those areas of our body and energy; we haven't learned how to exist there yet.

The Swiss cheese holes in our energy create holes in our energetic boundary. It is through these holes that others' emotions and energy enter our personal space. It is also where our energy and emotions leak out into the personal space of others.

What our energy looks like as "Swiss cheese"

Life without boundaries

When our energy boundary has been broken down over time—or if we, like so many people, never had a chance to learn what a real boundary looks and feels like—things can get a little messy. Without energy boundaries we feel the energy and emotions of others as if they are our own.

Without the right kind of boundaries in place we can easily feel overstimulated or overwhelmed by the world, or even by people we love and like to be around.

We can also have difficulty living up to our potential of helping to make the world a better place.

Energetic boundaries are a good thing!

Energetic boundaries are as important as physical boundaries when it comes to helping us feel safe in the world. We need energetic boundaries that reflect our clarity, our integrity, and the clear line that defines us from others.

Here are some other things we can experience when our boundaries are full of holes or missing altogether:

- ♥ Feeling the emotions, anxiety, pain, illness, or discomfort of others in our own body

- ♥ Feeling a lack of personal, energetic, or emotional autonomy

- ♥ Feeling the need to rely on emotional walls and angry forcefulness to feel safe or in control of our personal space or life

- ♥ Feeling drained by some individuals

- ♥ Difficulty determining if our emotions are our own

- ♥ Feeling like we are unable to stay grounded and rooted to the earth (when we are not grounded we might feel spacey, floaty, or clumsy)

- ♥ Feeling or sensing someone else in our personal, energetic, or emotional space even when they are not around us physically

- ♥ Avoiding life situations in which we don't feel safe or because we feel we are too sensitive to participate

- ♥ Regularly avoiding showing our amazing, unique, and awesome self because we don't feel safe doing so

- ♥ Feeling unsafe listening to or talking with someone with different ideas, beliefs, or political interests

Drawing your energetic Swiss cheese holes

The Swiss cheese holes in your energy change and evolve depending on your emotions, situation, sense of safety, and the people around you. Developing a sense of how to find and feel these holes can carry you a long way in terms of understanding where and how energy from others enters your personal space.

1. Gather your supplies, such as paper and colored pens or pencils.

2. Being as artsy as you would like, draw yourself in the center of the page. Add a circle around yourself to represent your energy boundary.

3. Get comfortable and calm your breathing. Keep your awareness in the center of your head, and feel into your inner song within your physical and energy bodies. Hang out there for a while.

4. Notice where in your being you do not feel your breath moving or inner song vibrating. Remember to explore with love and curiosity: these areas are part of your story and experience, and deserve respect and kindness.

5. Note the size of the area that is void of your inner song. What does it feel like to you? What shape is it? How does it change when you focus your awareness on the area? Do you feel or sense a color in this area?

6. On your paper, draw where on your body you feel this void and what you imagine it looks like based on what you feel when you listen to it.

Tip: Our Swiss cheese holes often shrink and begin to fill in with our own energy when we draw them or otherwise pay loving attention to them. It can be helpful to tune in using your inner senses after this exercise to notice how they have changed. Filling the holes within your boundary is a practice in itself: be patient and kind with yourself as you continue to work with this. Working with the exercise on pages 86–87 on a regular basis will also help you to feel more whole.

The Energetic Survival Spectrum

If you are like most people, you missed out on learning how to create a strong, loving, and compassionate boundary. Most of us seem to have skipped class that day.

Without the skills to create boundaries, we each learned how to create and rely on a whole spectrum of energy survival skills to help us feel safe in the world.

Throughout our life, each of us learns a wide range of ways to hold, move, and hide our energy to avoid picking up energy and emotions from others and all the other cosmic fly-by energy that is around us all of the time. I imagine it is much like running through an obstacle course all day long: dodging that, ducking under this, and doing our best not to let our energy just float away or merge with everything we run into.

However, these energetic survival skills are hard work. Even as great as they are, without a real energy boundary we still end up picking up stuff that is not ours and not feeling as comfortable with life as we could.

Before we get into how to create a real energy boundary, let's have a look at some of the creative things we have learned to do instead.

Merging

Merging is when we mingle our energy directly with someone else's energy and lose our energetic autonomy. There are many reasons we merge with individuals or groups of people. For example, it is common to merge with those we love.

At first merging can feel good, because all of those Swiss cheese holes that we walk around with are filled up. We might even feel a hopeful sense of love. But the downside of merging with someone else's energy is that pretty quickly we forget how to discern what is ours and what is theirs. It is a bit like if someone were to collect a bunch of stuff from their own desk and pile it in a heap with someone else's stuff from another desk. If the person left it that way long enough, they might not be able to tell right away whose stapler belongs to whom.

Sometimes we can unmerge with another pretty quickly, before our staplers get all mixed up. But most of the time we rely on some of our other energetic survival skills to try to push them out.

One way we do this is by creating an energy wall between ourselves and the person or situation that we are merged with. However, this simply hides a few aspects of who we are to others. It also limits the access we have to our own gifts and energy.

Two beings merging

Merging to resolve and problem-solve

Sometimes we also merge with those we have conflict with in an effort to resolve our issue with them.

Merging in an effort to resolve conflict

Merging for collaboration

We can even merge our energy just a little, like these two in the drawing who have merged their energy near their minds. Perhaps in this case it happened when they tried to collaborate on a solution or project. While it seems harmless, when we are merged with another, our energetic boundaries are nonexistent.

We can be collaborative and co-creative with others and still maintain our energy boundary; our work will be stronger for it!

A merging of minds

Merging with our pets

Some of us even merge with our pets to show affection, offer protection, or feel safe. Merging with our pet's energy can feel good at first but in the end it is not a good idea.

Merging with our cat's energy

Energy walls

Energy walls are sometimes confused with boundaries. They can feel like a boundary sometimes because they are so solid. But walls are created with tight jaws and fear, anger, or jealousy and little interest in cooperation. Boundaries are created with a relaxed body and jaw, love and compassion for ourselves and others, and the idea and hope of cooperation.

Walls and boundaries can sometimes work well together to keep us safe in a time of danger as a Plan B until we fully master creating solid boundaries.

When having a conversation with someone that we don't trust, we often rely on our energy walls to try to stay safe or to hide parts of ourselves that we don't want the other person to see or know about.

If we are feeling hurt, isolated, or unsure, sometimes we use giant walls that keep everyone's energy out in a forceful, angry way. We create these giant energy walls with very tight jaws and little breath.

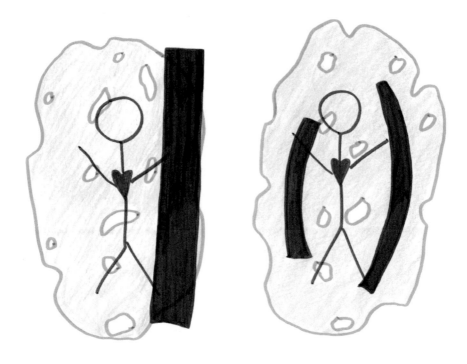

Two people using walls instead of boundaries

Walls that block everything out

Those on the other side of a giant wall can feel hurt, too, and left out. They can feel the angry, judgmental feelings behind our walls.

Using giant walls in place of boundaries

Internal and personal walls

Sometimes we even use energy walls to keep our own energy or a part of our personality walled off from parts of our body or energy. A very creative solution if we don't like a part of our body or have been hurt and are not ready to heal yet.

We might create an energy wall if we are trying to block out neck pain or don't like our voice

Dropping our boundaries to send our emotions

Sending our emotions to others, when it has been invited, is a natural human behavior that allows us to stay connected with those we love even when we are many miles apart.

However, if we come to rely on our ability to send our emotions on a regular basis, this can wear down our energy boundaries. This becomes especially problematic when we rely on sending our energy or emotions in place of speaking them.

In most life situations, when we simply radiate the emotions we are feeling, such as deep compassion or love, this is plenty.

The compassion we radiate will affect the situation in ways that honor both our boundaries and the boundaries of others. To envision what this looks like, let's think for a minute about how the Dalai Lama, Gandhi, and Mother Teresa simply radiate their love. They don't need to send it anywhere. Those who seek it will find it.

To help us visualize the difference between radiating emotions and sending emotions, let's look at a few examples of the latter.

When we send our emotions to another, we run into trouble because in order to send our emotions, we have to open a Swiss cheese hole in our boundary. In this case, even when the emotion is love, our boundary becomes breached when we send it. Think of how we send a letter in the mail: we cannot send a letter to someone without opening our front door and going to the mailbox.

All of our emotions can be wonderful, productive feelings, even anger, fear, and grief. However, when we intentionally send an emotion that belongs to us to someone else, our normal healthy emotion can become an energetic and emotional weapon.

Sending our feelings of certainty

If we have merged with someone's energy but don't like how it feels or know how to unmerge, sometimes we will get extra creative and send them some of our uncertainty, hoping they will get the message.

In reality, it is our responsibility to unmerge with the person so that we can each have our own space.

Two people merged and walled sending
uncertainty to each other

Sending anger to another

When we are really mad at someone and do not have our energetic boundary in place, we can unconsciously send emotional poison arrows. Without a clear boundary, our anger will travel right through our Swiss cheese holes into their Swiss cheese holes, and we will fill their space with our emotion. This is an unfortunate outcome to feeling normal, healthy emotions without clear boundaries in place.

Sometimes when our emotions are high with anger and we are in the heat of the moment, it can seem like a good idea to send someone our feelings. However, this action will only carry us that much farther from the healthy conflict resolution we would prefer in the long run.

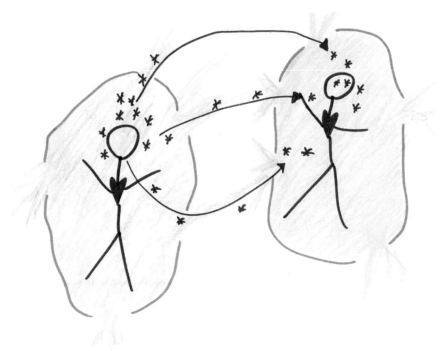

*One person sending anger through
their Swiss cheese holes into another
person's Swiss cheese holes*

Sending energy rather than speaking

As human beings it seems we have created an art form around sending "secret" poison arrows, especially when we are feeling one emotion while speaking another.

However, as good as we may be at this, the other person usually feels our truth, whether or not energetic boundaries are in place.

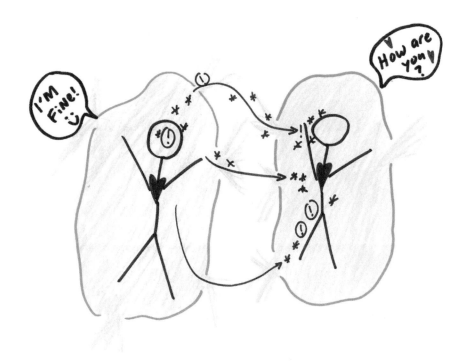

Saying one thing out loud while "secretly"
sending energetic poison arrows

Sending an energetic cord

At times we rely on sending an energetic cord to another. This cord can be large like a fire hose or small like a thin golden thread. Energy cords can behave much like a telephone cord, linking one being to another.

Cords can help us feel connected to those we love, but they can also feel uncomfortable or painful in our body. Much like sending energy to another, we are unable to maintain a clear and loving energetic boundary when we are also sending or receiving an energetic cord.

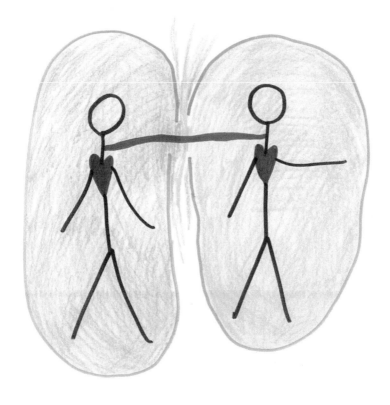

*Two people connected and communicating
with an energetic cord*

Letting our energy leave our body

For some people the best way to feel safe is to avoid scary and unpleasant-feeling things. Given that we have senses in both our physical and energy bodies, one way to avoid feeling something is to separate the two, thus decreasing the effectiveness of our sensory input. We can leave our body partially or completely.

When we are not in our body, we can feel spacey or dizzy or we may even trance out. We also get a little clumsy and bump into things. We might also have trouble concentrating.

When we leave our body even partially, the solid energy boundary that our body and energy create as a team is broken and our energy can leak. Just like when we get a paper cut and our body leaks a little.

Energy can also come into our space when we are not fully in our body.

Our energy leaving our body completely

When we partially leave our body,
we lose our boundary

THE ENERGETIC SURVIVAL SPECTRUM

Others' energy can get into our personal space when our energy leaves our body

Energy protection tools and leaving our body

One popular energy protection tool that many people use involves surrounding ourselves in a golden ball of energy. Although this tool can be useful, if we are not fully in our body to maintain our golden bubble of protection, it does not keep us as safe as we would like, and energy gets into our space.

*Golden bubbles really don't work for us
if we are not home to maintain them*

Shrinking

When we feel unsafe, we can also make our energy really small. It can feel like we have pulled in all of our energy close to our body. Our energy and the unique gifts we hold become concentrated when we shrink, as though we are folding in on ourselves. This prevents us from accessing all of our amazing qualities.

Two examples of shrinking our
energy close to our body

Internal shrinking

Sometimes we do this to make room for others because we feel they are more important or need more space than we do. Other times we may use shrinking to avoid a part of our body that hurts or that we don't like. We can also shrink our energy even tighter to focus on just one part of our body, or to leave a lot of room for others, or in hopes that others don't see us at all.

Shrinking our energy to hide
an aspect of our being

Overpowering another

When we are not feeling heard, or when we feel we need to justify who we are, our story, or what we stand for, at times we will use our energy to overpower another.

When we do this, our intentions are not always clear to those around us. To those we are overpowering, it can feel like we are bullying them. Or it can feel like we are trying to be affectionate even when we are not.

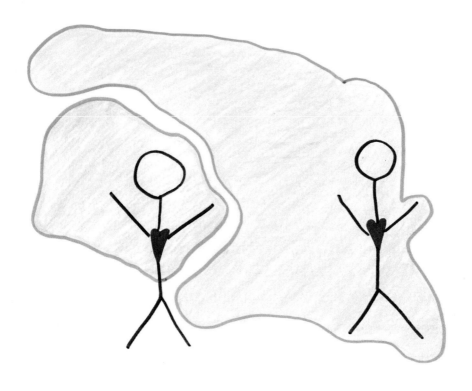

One person overpowering another,
who starts to leave their body

Inflating our energy

If we are feeling really brave and powerful, or if we feel we need to protect someone or overpower them, we can make our energy really big. Some fluctuations in the size of our energy and aura are normal: when we are in nature, or even when we are joyous or feeling angry, our energy naturally gets bigger. However, when we inflate our energy to overpower another, or to feel safe when we are unsure of ourselves, it is more of a survival skill than a healthy boundary.

When we inflate our energy too much, others may feel unsafe and shrink or leave their body. This creates a challenging situation in which collaboration and equality can have a hard time growing.

*One person inflates their energy,
a second person leaves their body,
and a third shrinks their energy*

Grounding through others

When we are having a hard time staying in our body or don't really know how to ground our energy to the earth to begin with, we often try to ground ourselves through another. This involves wrapping our energy around their grounding and following it into the earth.

When we ground ourselves through another person or a pet, we may not even know we are doing it. It may just feel good to be around them or think about them. However, to them it can feel suffocating.

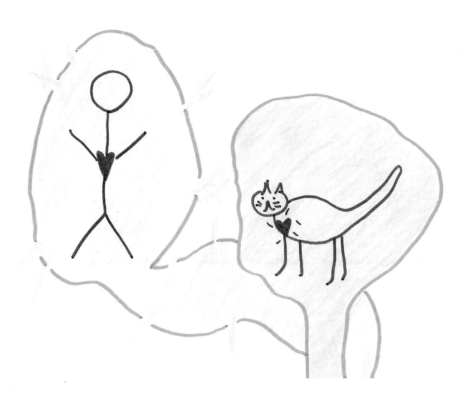

Grounding to the earth via a cat friend

Entangling

When we meet someone like us, who also needs help grounding or feeling safe, we can become entangled with their energy. It is a bit like two halves making up one whole: when we join forces and ground to the earth together, we can temporarily feel stronger.

Over time, our systems have a really hard time processing and integrating this kind of entanglement.

When we are entangled with someone, we can sense them even when they are not around. We might even see their face behind our closed eyes. We can also feel like we are falling in love when we really are not.

In this situation, our emotions become the other person's emotions and vice versa. Their pain and discomfort become ours. It can be very tricky to decide at any given moment who is who and what belongs to whom.

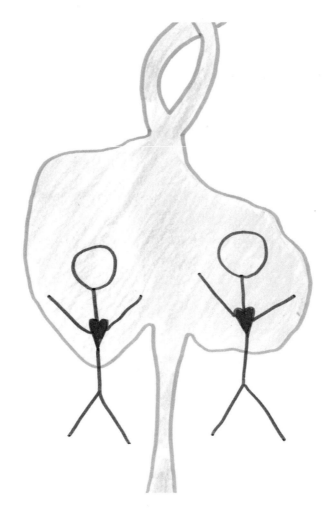

Entangling with another person and sharing a grounding to the earth

Creating an Energetic Boundary

Now that we have a good idea of some of the ways we blend and bend our energy when we do not have good energetic boundaries in place, let's have a look at how to create a basic energetic boundary.

To create an energy boundary, we need every element listed in the formula or our efforts will fall short. The process can take some time at first, but the more we practice, the better we get. Pretty soon we can find that we're adept enough to do an energy boundary check faster than we can check our Facebook feed.

Are you ready?

*To begin, let's revisit the
energetic boundary formula:*

Our body

+

Our energy

+

Our breath

+

Our presence in the present moment

+

Our love and gratitude

+

Our intent

_____

= Our energy boundary!

Creating your energetic boundary

This exercise combines everything we have covered so far, with the addition of a few new concepts to tie it all together.

1. Feel your physical body from inside your own skin. Feel into how many areas you can sense, simply by focusing your awareness and the direction of your breath. Remember to include your feet, knees, elbows, and the back side of your body.

2. Center your awareness into the center of your head.

3. Invite all of your energy fully back into your body and the present moment. Use your inner listening skills to see, feel, and sense the seamless connection between your energy and physical body and the unique inner song and vibration that this union creates.

4. Let your breath assist the natural deepening of the union of all that you are meeting the present moment. Notice your brilliant presence that is formed by this union. Your presence is the accumulation of your body, energy, love, and all that you are, in the here and now.

5. Visualize each inhale nourishing your presence within your core, much like how an ember in a fire brightens when offered the perfect amount of oxygen. Use all of your inner senses to see, feel, and sense your presence growing stronger.

6. With each inhale, allow your breath to create space within your body for your presence. With each exhale, allow your energy and presence to anchor, root and ground into your physical body.

7. With each inhale, weave your love and gratitude with your presence. Include the love and gratitude you have for who you are, your personal learning and growing, and your potential, as well as all that you appreciate in the world like fresh air and clean water.

8. With each exhale, intend to extend your presence throughout the whole of your physical and energetic body, filling your whole being with your unique and divine essence combined with your love and gratitude for yourself and those around you. Continue extending your presence, until you feel yourself reach your own natural stopping point. This is the natural boundary of where your vibration ends and the rest of the world begins. Ideally this boundary lies about 3 feet from the edge of your physical body, front to back, side to side, and above and below you.

9. Feel this new energetic boundary that you have created. Notice how it moves with you effortlessly. Notice how it is not something outside of you, nor is it a separation between you and the world, but rather it is you, embodied fully in the here and now.

10. Be gentle with yourself as you practice interacting with others with your new boundary in place. As often as needed, feel your breath feeding your presence and extend your presence to the edge of your boundary with each exhale.

Tip: The following mantra can be helpful in remembering the steps of this exercise: I Center. I Breathe in, I feed my presence. I Exhale, I extend my presence. With each breath, my boundary is strengthened and becomes more loving, creating space for me while honoring everyone around me.

Voilà! You with a boundary. You have created a basic energy boundary that will help you feel more like yourself again. Nice job!

Developing a Personal Practice

The energy boundary you have just created is a perfect foundation on which to build even richer energy boundaries that will help you feel safe even in difficult situations. It can take some practice to mend all the layers of Swiss cheese holes we find in our space. But this basic boundary will help you feel better in the meantime.

Once you get really good at this, you can quickly just puff yourself up like a blowfish—poof!—and have a solid energy boundary.

Trying out a new energy boundary

As you practice creating an energy boundary, it might feel a little weird or different at first, especially when you are around other people. It might be helpful to begin by sitting with your favorite pet friend. See what it takes to maintain your boundary even when you are petting them.

If you don't have a pet, you can try the same thing with a tree!

If you feel yourself merging, using another to ground, or using other energy survival skills, go easy on yourself. Creating a lasting energy boundary takes practice! You can and will get this. If you stumble and resort to using old energy survival skill habits, just start again, create a new energy boundary using the formula, and you will be on your way again.

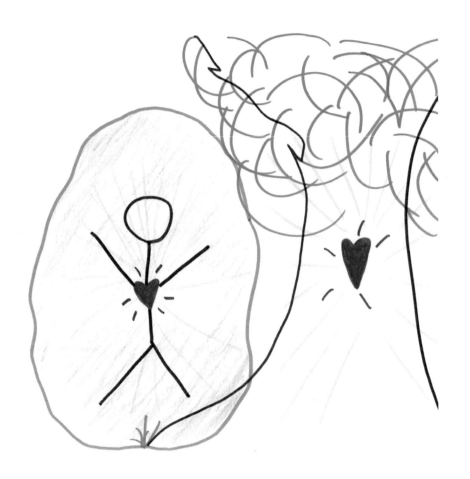

*You can practice maintaining
your boundary with a tree*

Giving yourself regular energy-boundary Tuneups

When starting a new boundary practice, it can be helpful to tune up your energy boundary on a daily basis.

Once you feel secure in the steps and formula for creating an energetic boundary (see pages 86 and 87), give yourself short boundary tuneups as needed. Tuneups are especially helpful as you prepare for a busy day or meeting, or before interacting with challenging situations and people.

Here is a short, sweet energetic boundary tuneup:

1. Notice and connect with your calm, steady, natural breath.

2. Center your awareness into the center of your head.

3. Allow your breath to help you reconnect your whole being to the present moment.

4. Notice areas in your body and energy that you can feel your presence and areas where you cannot.

5. Focus your natural breath to feed your presence and extend it as you fill your whole being with your own presence. Front and back, to the left and right of you, above and below you.

6. With each exhale, root your presence into your physical body. Allow your presence to extend into every ounce of your being, until you feel the natural stopping point at which your energy ends and the rest of the world begins.

7. Finish by noticing the strength of your replenished energetic boundary all around you, holding you and creating a safe container for all of who you are.

*Maintaining a boundary around someone
who is having a hard time*

When things get messy, be the Gouda

When we are around others that are feeling and emitting heavy emotions, we might feel the need to do some of the energetic gymnastics we talked about earlier.

Stay strong, let your energy sink even deeper into your bones by taking a few deeper breaths, and remember your brilliance. After a little practice you will find it easier to stay in your own space. And during the most difficult and trying of times, remember: be the Gouda, not the Swiss.

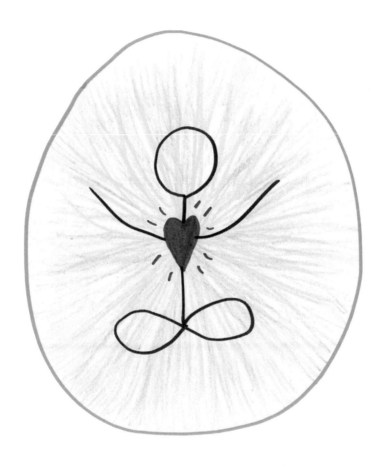

Be the Gouda

Hungry for more information?

This book focuses on the foundational portion of a larger body of work. Four more books are in the works, each with a specific audience: a book for healers and caregiving professionals, one for energy-sensitive empaths, a very special book for sensitive children, and a follow-up to this 101 book on creating loving energetic boundaries for challenging situations.

Meanwhile, please check out my blog, where you will find articles and updates on upcoming books, links to audio recordings of the exercises in this book, as well as more resources on energetic boundaries.

www.JoannaSchmidt.com

About the Author

JOANNA SCHMIDT has been an empathic and energy-sensitive person her whole life. Growing up a sensitive kid was challenging but presented a wonderful opportunity to grow and learn.

In 2015 Joanna celebrated her twentieth year in full-time private practice in the healing arts. She now sees much of her healing work with others as part of a larger continuum: for her part, she aims to help others feel empowered and equipped to create the healing they are here to create and reach those who need their unique gifts the most.

Joanna and her beloved husband, Steve, auto mechanic extraordinaire, live in Bellingham, Washington, with their animal family: Sue, a black lab-ish dog who loves a good run in the woods, and Bernard, a chow-bulldog mix who can bark louder than any other dog they know.

Joanna offers private healing sessions, mentoring, and workshops in energetic boundaries, animal communication, and shamanic healing and practice.

www.JoannaSchmidt.com

Special thanks to …

My childhood friend Mindy Fitch, word and grammar midwife, for all her help with editing; Terry Drussel, graphic design goddess of Fat Black Squirrel Studio, for the creation of the book cover; Katrina Svoboda Johnson for her friendship and for lending a hand with fine tuning my doodles and artwork; Angie Lokotz of ElfElm Publishing for her handy work in formatting and helping to shape my words into a real book; Burke Mulvany of Sound House Services for offering his audio recording skills, ideas, and amazing musical talents in our collaborations and for recording the exercises in this book; my loving husband, Steve, for spending tireless hours proofreading copy after copy of this book, and for his endless love and encouragement; and my mom, Phyllis, for being the best mother and teacher one could hope for.

37845510R00060

Made in the USA
Middletown, DE
03 March 2019